published in the united states by kaleidoscope kids, llc

visit us at www.readkaleidoscope.com

kaleidoscope, *kids bibles reimagined*

library of congress cataloging-in-publication data is available upon request
ISBN: 979-8-9851532-2-4

cover art by courtney kassner @crewandco
logo design by morgan carter @bymorgancarter
editing by laurie sibley

To Stephen, Stewart, Charles, and Pace.
Thank you for helping me
navigate life in a broken world.

WELCOME TO KALEIDOSCOPE

First of all, thank you for picking up a copy of Kaleidoscope! We are glad to have you. In the following pages, you'll experience the Bible in a whole new way.

Kaleidoscope was borne from the need to provide a fun, engaging, age-appropriate retelling of the Bible for elementary-aged children transitioning from "little kid" Bibles to adult translations.

At Kaleidoscope, we're producing single volumes for every book of the Bible. They're designed to read like chapter books, so you'll turn pages and look forward with anticipation to the next volume.

But don't let the fact that we are focused on kids deter you if you are a "big kid!" Good children's books are almost always as good for adults as they are for kids.

Get excited! In the pages that follow, you'll see God's wonderful good news. Our prayer is that His kindness, gentleness, and love will melt our hearts and make us more like Jesus.

The Kaleidoscope Team

Far From Home will encourage you, make you laugh, and make you cry tears of hope-filled joy as you read this retelling of the book of Daniel with your kids. All of the Bible, including the book of Daniel, shows us who God is and points us to Jesus, and *Far From Home* does an excellent job at doing just that as it retells the book of Daniel in a clear and accessible way for young readers. I am so thankful for Kaleidoscope and the many ways these books have fostered family discipleship opportunities and shaped our family's bible reading and conversations around our kitchen table.

-Courtney Tracy, blogger and author of the upcoming devotional: *Putting Jesus First: A 21-Day Devotional Journey Through Colossians*

Blessing, obedience, and God's favor...Kaleidoscope makes these themes come alive in their engaging retelling of the book of Daniel. Young readers (and their parents) are sure to take away a revelation of importance of choosing obedience and living a life of godliness.

-Haley Ortego, owner and founder of The Brave Mama Co. (@thebravemamaco)

I'm so thankful for a kids' Bible that not only offers my children more clarity, but that does the same for me as I read aloud to them! This is a fantastic resource for kids and parents alike.

-Hunter Beless, Founder and Executive Director of Journeywomen *&* the host of the Journeywomen Podcast

CREATORS

Chris Ammen is the founder of Kaleidoscope and a Children's Pastor in Chattanooga. He has a BA and M.Ed. in Elementary Education as well as an M.Div. from Covenant Seminary. When not writing, Chris loves spending time with his wife, Sarah, and their four awesome kiddos!

Garyfallia Leftheri studied French Professional Translation, but her passion for drawing drove her to ORNERAKIS School of Cartoon and Animation in Athens, Greece, and later on to the University of Glamorgan in UK, where she studied Stop Motion Animation. She lives in Athens with her husband and their twins and she works as an illustrator for educative and children's books. She loves sewing kids' toys, cooking and reading fairy tales.

TABLE OF
CONTENTS

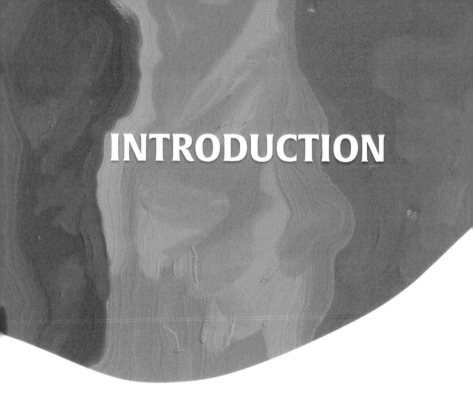

INTRODUCTION

I've always loved puppet shows. If you've ever seen a good one, you know what it's like—the puppets seem to have a life all their own. It's *so* fun!

The book of Daniel is like a puppet show where God is the puppeteer. This puppet show, however, is very sad.

You see, for centuries God warned His people, Israel, that judgment was coming for their sin. But did they listen? Not at all!

So, God took the strings of a "puppet" country called Babylon. He allowed the evil Babylonians to steal God's people from their homes in Jerusalem. As a result, most Israelites soon lived in Babylon, far from what they knew as "home," both in location and morality.

The situation seemed hopeless for Israel. Babylonians were known for their evil ways. They wanted nothing to do with God and treated His people horribly.

But God had plans to strengthen Israel, even in the middle of one of their most embarrassing moments.

This is where Daniel comes in.

Daniel was just a teenage boy when his family left for Babylon. But, God blessed him with extraordinary wisdom. As you'll soon read, he quickly became one of the most important men in Babylon, even though he was from Israel. He won the respect of the leaders and was the person God spoke to the most during this period of time.

Most of all, Daniel gave the people of Israel hope that God had not left them and that faithfulness was still worth it.

Today we need Daniel more than ever. While we aren't in the same situation as the Israelites, we still face the values of Babylon every day. Daniel helps us know what following God looks like when most of the world does not believe in Him. In fact, according to most researchers, the number of evangelical Christians is less than 10% worldwide! So, whether you feel it yet or not, it's going to take a lot of wisdom to follow Jesus for the rest of your life!

Daniel helps our faith grow as we see that God is in control of all things, even when life feels crazy. He is the puppeteer of His creation. He is in charge of all kings and kingdoms. He raises up those who honor Him and humbles those who think too highly of their own power.

Most of all, Daniel points us to Jesus, who will finally and fully defeat all evil and bring His people to their eternal, forever home.

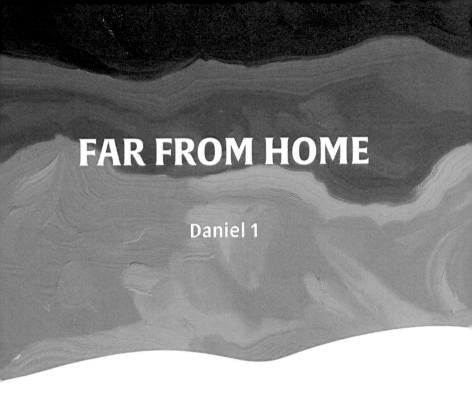

FAR FROM HOME

Daniel 1

If only everyone had been paying attention, the book of Daniel might have never happened. But it did. And even though it's a tragedy of sorts, it's good because God was at work.

You see, for years, prophets (like Isaiah and Jeremiah) warned people that God wouldn't put up with their sinful ways much longer. Eventually, out of love for Israel (another name for God's people), He used another country to discipline them.

That country was known as Babylon.

Here's how it happened...

1

In the year 605 BC, a man named Jehoiakim was the king of Israel. However, he only led for two years because, during his third year, God sent the king of Babylon, Nebuchadnezzar (pronounced Neb-ah-kahd-nez-er), to capture Israel and take them far from home.

That's right! The book of Daniel is about one BIG kidnapping, which is also known as "exile."

Nebuchadnezzar took thousands of Israelites back to Babylon. God's people went from the Promised Land, where they enjoyed the protection of God, to a land far, far away. In Babylon, God was the last thing on anyone's mind. What a sad, sad turn of events!

It wasn't long until Nebuchadnezzar met the royal family of Israel. He grew especially interested in the smartest and brightest of the children.

You see, Nebuchadnezzar wanted these children to learn the language of the Babylonians. He tried to teach them all about their new home. He even gave them super-yummy food to eat!

After three years of learning, the most promising Israelite children went to work for the king. Among these children were Azariah, Mishael, Hananiah, and Daniel.

But these would not be their names for much longer. Nebuchadnezzar's assistants changed their names from Israelite to Babylonian names. This was no small matter. In fact, it was a way for Nebuchadnezzar to remove some of their identity as the people of God. They'd already lost their homes and familiar friends and places. Now, they'd lost the one thing they'd had since birth!

Their new names were: Shadrach, Meshach, Abednego, and Daniel was known as Belteshazzar (for our purposes, though, we'll keep calling Daniel by his birth name).

These names may sound very unusual, but they were music to Nebuchadnezzar's ears. Each name was an insult to the One True God, or a celebration of one of his pretend gods.

Daniel, though, would not play Nebuchadnezzar's foolish games. When the king wanted the boys to eat and drink mouth-watering Babylonian food and wine, Daniel knew he wasn't honoring God.

So, Daniel asked one of the king's helpers to bring him different food. But the helper refused, saying, "I'm not so sure about that. If you don't eat the king's rich, savory food, your health will suffer. It will become obvious to everyone that you've disobeyed the king."

Daniel replied, "Let's put this to the test. For ten days, give us only vegetables and water. Then, see how we look next to the other children who eat the rich, savory food of the king."

This was quite a risky request! How would a bunch of lettuce-eaters look compared to those who ate extravagant meals after a week and a half?

But you should know that this story is about much more than what Daniel ate. In fact, this is how the whole book of Daniel goes:

1. Daniel faces a challenge.
2. Daniel honors God.
3. God prepares Daniel for an even greater challenge.

As you'll see in a few chapters, this vegetable diet was only the beginning of Daniel's problems.

Miraculously, after ten days, Daniel and his friends were healthier and stronger than the children who ate the rich, savory food. God had clearly protected and strengthened them!

The four boys grew in wisdom and knowledge as they lived in the king's palace. God honored their faithfulness. Daniel even gained the ability to understand dreams (this skill will become quite useful in just a few pages)!

Nebuchadnezzar called Daniel, Shadrach, Meshach, and Abednego to his chambers at the end of their three years of learning.

"When it comes to wisdom and understanding, there is not a single person in all my kingdom who's like these four boys," the king declared.

And so, Daniel, Shadrach, Meshach, and Abednego were given places of honor in Babylon. They worked for the king and lived in his palace.

But would they stay faithful to God? Day after day, they were now far from home in a land that seemed ready to shake their faith at every turn in the road.

Kaleidoscope Corner
The Name Game

In this first chapter of Daniel, our friends receive a name change from King Nebuchadnezzar. This was a BIG deal because it was about a lot more than just a name. The king was trying to slowly mold his star students into the ways of the Babylonians.

Here's what their names meant before and after the change. Notice that some of the names had more than one meaning.

Daniel, which means "God is my judge," became Belteshazzar, which means "O Lady (another name for the wife of the Babylonian god Bel), protect the king!"

Hananiah, which means "Yahweh is gracious," became Shadrach, which means "I am very fearful (of God)" or "The command of Aku (the Babylonian moon god)."

Mishael, which means "Who is what God is?" became Meshach, which means "I am of little account" or "Who is like (the Babylonian god) Aku?"

Azariah, which means "Yahweh is a helper," became Abednego, which means "The servant of the shining one (the Babylonian god Nebo)."

Of course, these new names meant very little in the long run. God knew each of these boys by name. In fact, the most important name they had was "child of God."

VANISHING KINGDOMS

Daniel 2

Have you ever had a bad dream? They can be scary and confusing and often quite bewildering. Well, Nebuchadnezzar had quite the nightmare one evening, and it left him terribly troubled.

So, the king called the brightest people in all of Babylon to his palace, demanding, "I need one of you to tell me what my dream was about. If you can't, I will kill you all and burn your houses to ashes."

Clearly, the king was quite grumpy and in no mood for any funny business!

"But," Nebuchadnezzar continued, "if you can tell me the meaning of my dream, I will reward you with gifts and great honor."

The wise men answered, "Tell us your dream, and we will help you make sense of it."

Their request seemed reasonable enough. But remember, Nebuchadnezzar was far from reasonable.

"No, no, no," the king replied. "You must tell me what happened in my dream *and* tell me what it means."

"There's no man on earth who can do that. No king has ever asked his servants to do such an impossible task!" the men answered.

At this, Nebuchadnezzar grew furious and sentenced all the wise men of Babylon to death. But, just in time, the wise men remembered someone who could help.

Daniel.

The wise men pleaded with Daniel to assist them. Fortunately, he agreed.

But, before he went, Daniel asked his friends, Shadrach, Meshach, and Abednego, for help. "Please pray to God for help and mercy. The wise men of Babylon are in great trouble, and we will likely die with them if this goes poorly."

Then, the mystery of Nebuchadnezzar's dream was made plain as day to Daniel, and he blessed the God of heaven for providing, saying, "Praise God! He alone gives kings power and takes their power away."

Oh no! This dream sounds like it might make the king even grumpier!

Then Daniel went to Arioch, who Nebuchadnezzar had asked to destroy the wise men, begging, "Do not kill them! Instead, bring me to the king. I will show him his dream and what it means."

Imagine for a moment that you are Arioch. If Daniel cannot satisfy the king, you might end up dead yourself! But God gave Arioch the confidence to trust Daniel. So he brought Daniel to Nebuchadnezzar's chambers.

The king greeted Daniel, asking, "Are you able to tell me my dream and what it means? None of the other wise men have been able to."

Daniel answered, "There's nobody wise enough for that task. But there is a God in heaven who is mighty and able to help."

Daniel was correct. The king's request was quite outrageous!

Daniel began, "You saw a great creature-like statue. It was extremely frightening to you. Its head was made of gold, and its chest was wrapped in silver, with thighs carved from bronze and legs molded from iron. Its feet were made of iron and clay.

"As you watched with terror, a stone struck the statue's feet and broke them into pieces. Then the iron, the clay, the bronze, the silver, and the gold all collapsed and became like husks of wheat — carried off by the wind as if the statue had never been there in the first place.

"But while the statue disappeared, the stone grew into a mountain and filled the whole earth."

The dream was just as Nebuchadnezzar remembered it.

Daniel continued, "And now, this is what your dream means: God has given you power and might and glory. He gave you much to rule over, but you are merely the head of gold.

"You, O king, are great... but your kingdom will not last forever. Another kingdom made of silver will come after you. But that kingdom will not last either. Next, one of bronze will arise, and then one of iron. Finally, a kingdom of clay and iron will come. Each of these kingdoms will be weaker than the one before it.

"But God, who rules from heaven, has a kingdom that will never fail. It will crush all the other kingdoms and bring them to an end. God's kingdom will stand as our eternal kingdom, our forever home. His kingdom is the stone that crushes the statue, and grows into a great mountain, covering the whole earth."

With this news, King Nebuchadnezzar fell on his face. Was he mad? Was he sad? Would he lash out at Daniel?

Instead, the king thanked Daniel. "Truly, your God is the God of all the gods and the Lord of all the kings. He knows all things and has made known to you the mystery of my dream."

Then the king gave Daniel many honors and gifts and even made him a ruler over Babylon, putting him in charge of Babylon's wise men.

Daniel also asked that his friends, Shadrach, Meshach, and Abednego, receive better jobs.

Years earlier, the prophet Jeremiah encouraged Israel to pray for and work for the good of the city where they found themselves while in exile.

It seemed that God remembered this encouragement and, with His mighty, skillful, and wise hand, guided Daniel and his friends as they lived in a city set against them.

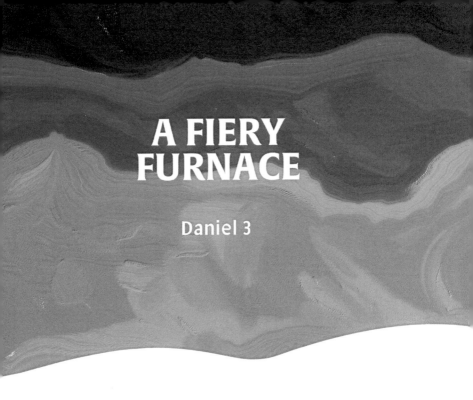

A FIERY FURNACE

Daniel 3

Daniel had just done the impossible: God gave him the ability to see into Nebuchadnezzar's dream. More than that, though, Daniel told Nebuchadnezzar what his dream meant. After all this, you would think Nebuchadnezzar would find himself bowed down before God in worship.

But that was not the case.

Instead, Nebuchadnezzar built a massive 90-foot tall statue of pure gold from head to foot. The message, of course, was that Nebuchadnezzar believed his kingdom would never be replaced by another.

Then the king gathered all of his big, important government officials to see the statue he'd made. He wanted everyone to know that his kingdom was the only one worthy of their service, allegiance, and, well... worship.

Upon seeing the statue, the king's assistant declared, "Whoever refuses to bow down and worship this golden statue will be thrown into a burning, red hot, fiery furnace."

In other words, if you do not obey the king, you're a dead man walking. So what would Daniel and his friends do?

Just then, a group of magicians known as Chaldeans approached the king. "O king, did you not say that everyone in all of your kingdom must worship this magnificent golden statue which you have made? Did you not say that if someone refused to, they would wind up in the burning, red hot, fiery furnace?"

Can't you just picture the smug grin on the magicians' faces as the king nodded back in approval?

"Well, king, we would just like to point out that those boys, the Israelite ones — Shadrach, Meshach, and Abednego, won't worship the golden statue."

King Nebuchadnezzar boiled in rage. "Bring those boys to me at once!" he commanded.

When the boys arrived, Nebuchadnezzar scolded them. "Is it true that you will not serve my gods or worship the golden statue that I made? You know what will happen if you do not do as I've asked, right?! Tell me, what god will save you then?"

What would they do? Certainly, death awaited the boys within a millisecond of entering the furnace!

Shadrach, Meshach, and Abednego answered the king confidently, saying, "Our God will protect us. So do with us what you please."

At this, Nebuchadnezzar was enraged. "Turn the furnace up seven times hotter than usual!"

Then, Nebuchadnezzar ordered that the boys be tied up with rope and thrown into the furnace with all their clothing and hats still on their heads. The king's servants did just what he asked. But, because it was much hotter than usual, even the servants who brought the boys died as the flames leaped out of the furnace. How would the boys survive?

Just then, something remarkable happened: something that could only happen because God controls all things, including burning, red hot, fiery furnaces.

The king looked in the furnace and declared with great confusion, "Did we not throw three boys, bound with a rope into the fire to die? Why do I see four men, unbound, walking in the middle of the fire unharmed? And why is it that the fourth man looks like the son of the gods?"

Nebuchadnezzar declared, "Shadrach, Meshach, and Abednego, servants of the Most High God, come out of there at once!"

And just like that, the boys emerged unharmed from the furnace. Not a hair on their heads was burned, and their clothing and hats didn't even smell of fire.

The king was astonished, saying to the boys, "Blessed be the God of Shadrach, Meshach, and Abednego. He sent His angel and saved His servants, who trusted Him. They did not listen to my command but instead honored their own God!

"Therefore, anyone who speaks against the God of Shadrach, Meshach, and Abednego will be killed, along with their family. I've never seen any other god in all creation who can rescue quite like this!"

The king continued, "Peace to everyone! How great is the Most High God! He has done mighty wonders. His kingdom is everlasting and endures from generation to generation!"

God had met Nebuchadnezzar, and Nebuchadnezzar had met God.

One question bears asking at this point. Who was the fiery furnace for? Was it to strengthen Shadrach, Meshach, and Abednego? Perhaps. Was it to bring Nebuchadnezzar one step closer to not only saying the Most High God is "their God," but that he is also "Nebuchadnezzar's God?"

It seems that both of these may be true. As we will see, this fiery, golden day was all a part of God's rescue plan for Nebuchadnezzar.

THE DEW OF HEAVEN

Daniel 4

That last chapter was a stunning turn of events, right?!
God had Nebuchadnezzar squarely in His sights, drawing
his heart to the true King.

But, just as everything seemed to settle down from the
fiery furnace and the golden statue, it all happened again!
Nebuchadnezzar had another startling dream, and he
called all the wise men of Babylon to his palace once more.

Nebuchadnezzar explained the dream to the smartest of
the smart people in his kingdom, but, of course, none
could tell him exactly what his dream meant.

At last, Daniel (you saw that coming, didn't you?!) came in,
and the king began to tell his trusty servant the dream.

"I saw a tree," Nebuchadnezzar began. "The tree grew large and strong until its top reached to heaven, and everyone from one end of the earth to the other could see it.

"Its leaves were beautiful and full of fruit, and it had enough food for the whole world. Even the animals found rest beneath its shade and homes under its branches.

"But then, a holy one came down from heaven, proclaiming, 'Chop down this tree at once! Cut its branches! Scatter the animals! But leave the tree's stump in the earth, wrapped in iron and bronze and yet surrounded by the dew of heaven. And let seven periods of time pass over the tree.

"'Then all will know that the Most High rules the kingdom of men.'"

Nebuchadnezzar trembled as he looked Daniel in the eye. This mighty man had been reduced to a puddle as he asked, "Tell me what this means. Nobody else can, but you are able because the Spirit of God is in you."

Daniel's heart raced, and his mind spun. But Daniel knew what he must do. So he told Nebuchadnezzar what the dream meant. "The tree, with its huge trunk, beautiful leaves, delicious fruit, and homes for animals, is... you."

You could have heard a pin drop in the palace.

"Your greatness has grown, and your power reaches to the ends of the earth. But it's not right that a man like yourself should have so much power.

"So, the holy one in heaven came saying, 'Chop down the tree and destroy it, but let it be wet with the dew of heaven, and let it live among the beasts of the field for seven periods of time.'"

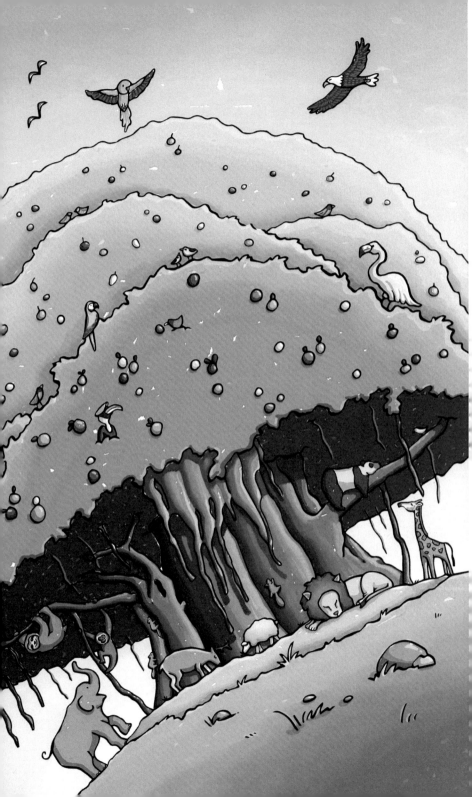

"So king," Daniel continued, "you have to leave your people and live as a beast. You will eat grass like an ox until you know that the Most High God rules over every kingdom.

"O king, I beg you to obey the Lord, show mercy to the hurting, and perhaps God will allow you to rule for longer."

Twelve long months went by after the dream, and nothing more happened. Then one day, Nebuchadnezzar was walking on the roof of his palace, saying, "Isn't Babylon glorious? I've built it with my power and glory."

While these words were still falling from the king's lips, a voice came from heaven just as Daniel said it would. "O King Nebuchadnezzar," the voice spoke, "your kingdom has left you. For seven periods of time, you will leave your people and eat grass like an ox until you know that the Most High God rules all the kingdoms of the world."

Immediately, it happened just as the voice said.

Nebuchadnezzar was taken from his home and ate grass like an ox. His body was wet with the dew of heaven, a constant reminder of God's presence, until his hair grew as long as eagles' feathers, and his nails were like birds' claws. It was as if God showed the king that he had been behaving more like an animal than a man!

As Nebuchadnezzar's strange animal period drew to a close, he lifted his eyes to heaven and blessed the Most High God. He praised Him and honored the One who truly lives and rules forever, saying, "His power is forever. His kingdom is eternal. He is in control of all things."

At this, Nebuchadnezzar returned to his people. Once again, majesty and splendor returned to him.

Nebuchadnezzar spoke. "I praise and honor the King of heaven, for everything He does is right. But He will humble those who walk in pride, like me."

Could it be that God's kindness had softened the once cruel Nebuchadnezzar? Indeed, it appeared so! God loved Nebuchadnezzar enough to bring him low.

Like, literally... He made him live like a beast, on all fours, to get his attention. Our God works in incredible ways to call His children home!

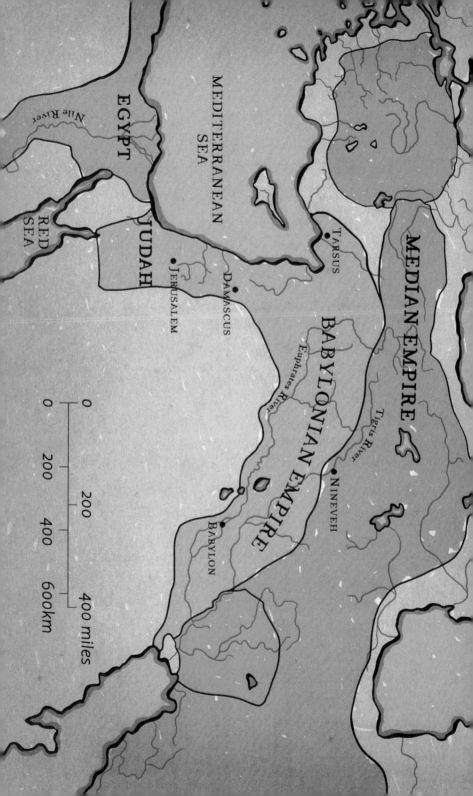

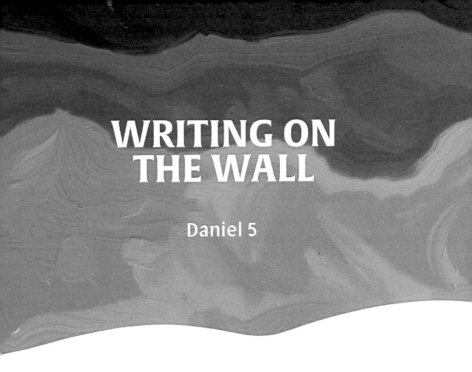

WRITING ON THE WALL

Daniel 5

Some time passed, and another king rose to power in Babylon. His name was King Belshazzar—which sounds a bit like Daniel's Babylonian name, Belteshazzar. But, rest assured—they were nothing alike!

The Bible says Belshazzar was the son of Nebuchadnezzar, but history tells us that this wasn't *exactly* true.

Belshazzar was not actually Nebuchadnezzar's son. Instead, he wanted to be just like the power-hungry Nebuchadnezzar. So Belshazzar just called him his father. Strange, I know!

One night, King Belshazzar and his friends were drinking wine from fancy gold and silver cups that Nebuchadnezzar stole from the temple in Jerusalem.

Suddenly, the strangest of strange things happened.

Across the room, the fingers of a human hand mysteriously appeared and began writing on the walls of the king's palace!

Belshazzar's blood ran cold, and his face turned a ghostly pale shade of white. His arms and legs went limp, and he even pooped his pants (you read that right!).

In a panic, Belshazzar called the wise men of Babylon to help. "Whoever can tell me what this means will be dressed in fine purple clothing, have gold draped from their neck, and serve alongside me as the king of Babylon!"

But none of the wise men could make any sense of the writing.

The blood drained from Belshazzar's face once again as the queen of Babylon consoled him, "O king, do not let this bother you. Surely, your kingdom will live forever." But, of course, these were false promises made with no knowledge or respect for God.

The queen continued, "There's a man who has the wisdom of the gods. He has understanding beyond any earthly ruler. Your 'father' Nebuchadnezzar made him one of the chiefs in Babylon. His name is Daniel. You should ask him. He can help."

So Belshazzar called for Daniel. When Daniel arrived, Belshazzar asked, "You're one of the men from Judah, correct?"

Daniel nodded as if to say "yes." The king was likely surprised that someone outside Babylon had such wisdom.

The king then caught Daniel up to speed. He told him about the mysterious hand and the offer to the wise men of purple clothing, gold, and a spot as a fellow ruler of Babylon. He also told Daniel that none of the wise men could tell him anything about the handwriting.

"Keep your gifts—the purple, the gold, and the kingship. I will read the writing and tell you what it means," Daniel replied, unimpressed by the king's money and power. Daniel knew he needed to explain something much greater in value than gold to the king.

"King, the Most High God set Nebuchadnezzar as the king of Babylon. God gave him greatness, glory, and majesty. Because of his greatness, everyone, everywhere trembled with fear. He killed whoever he wanted. He lifted people to power if he wished and destroyed the lives of those he hated.

"But when he did this, God took his glory. He was made to live as a wild animal in a field. God brought him low so he would know that the Lord is in charge of all things, including kings.

"When Nebuchadnezzar understood that the Most High God is the true ruler of all the kingdoms of the earth, he was brought back to living as a human."

All of this was common knowledge by this point. People don't often live like animals and become humans again without that story making the rounds!

Then Daniel looked at Belshazzar sternly, saying, "You, Belshazzar, are making the same mistakes as Nebuchadnezzar. You have not humbled your heart, even though you know what happened to your 'father.'

"The writing on the palace wall reads, 'Mene, Mene, Tekel, and Parsin.'"

These are all measures of weight common to Babylonians. Mene meant "numbered," tekel meant "weighed," and parsin meant "divided." The king knew the words well, but he could not understand the message because his heart had grown hard.

Daniel explained, "Mene - God has numbered your days and will bring your kingdom to an end. Tekel - God has weighed your leadership as a king and found that you have not measured up. Parsin - God will divide your kingdom and give it to the kingdoms of the Medes and Persians."

Then, even though Daniel refused, Belshazzar dressed him in fine purple, a chain of gold was placed around his neck, and the king declared that Daniel was equal in power to him.

We aren't quite sure what happened in the hours that followed. But, by the following day, Belshazzar had been killed.

In his place, Darius the Mede took over the kingdom at the age of 62.

A DEN OF LIONS

Daniel 6

It wasn't long before Darius the Mede, the new king of Babylon, devised his plan for ruling his new land. He gave 120 people the job of "satrap." These people were to watch over the land and make sure everyone obeyed the law. These satraps reported to three high officials.

Daniel was named as one of those high officials.

To nobody's surprise, Daniel became the most celebrated of the high officials. Darius even planned to make him ruler over the entire kingdom. How do you think the other leaders felt about that?

They were jealous. Very, very jealous!

So, the satraps and high officials looked for something—anything—wrong with Daniel. But they could find nothing. Daniel was without fault because he was faithful to God. So, the satraps devised a wicked, cruel plan to trick Daniel.

Darius, you should know, was like all the other kings. He thought quite highly of himself, just like Nebuchadnezzar and Belshazzar. So, when the satraps approached Darius with an idea to increase his power, he welcomed it with open arms.

"King, let's make a new law," the satraps suggested. "Anyone who prays to anyone but you will be thrown into a den of bloodthirsty lions. If you set this law in place, it cannot be changed!"

Not knowing the story behind the plan, Darius made their sneaky idea into an unchangeable law.

When Daniel heard about the new law, he was not discouraged. You read that right—*not* discouraged! Instead, he did the same thing he did each day. He went to his house three times every day, faced Jerusalem, got down on his knees, prayed, and gave thanks to God.

I'd imagine you can guess what happened next! The men who suggested the new law followed Daniel and saw him praying to God in his home. Then they marched back to the king's palace to deliver the news.

"O king, your law has already been broken! Daniel, one of the men from Judah, apparently does not pay attention to you. Instead, he prays to his God three times each day. Now, you must throw him to those growly, hungry lions!"

However, Darius was nowhere near as excited about this news as the others. He loved Daniel and even planned to make him the leader of the whole region of Babylon.

But, in the kingdom of the Medes and Persians, once a law was made, it could not be changed. So Darius had to do the very thing he hated. He commanded Daniel to come near, and threw him into a den of lions with the hopeful words, "May your God, who you serve, save you!"

Then, to make sure there was no escape, he set a stone against the opening to the den. It was as if they were building a tomb for Daniel's all-but-certain death.

The king tossed and turned in his bed all night. He was saddened by what he'd done to Daniel. It didn't seem fair. Deep down inside, he hoped that Daniel would survive.

In the morning, as the sun crept over the horizon, the king ran to the den, calling out, "Daniel, Daniel! Has your God saved you?"

Then, to everyone's surprise, Daniel shouted back, "O king! Live forever! My God sent His angel to shut the lions' mouths. I don't even have a scratch!"

Then Darius brought Daniel out of the den. No harm was done to Daniel because he had trusted in God to save him. The king was exceedingly glad! But Darius was not done with the lions... not quite yet!

Darius called the men who'd accused Daniel and threw them, and their families, into the den. In an instant, the lions pounced on them, crushing their bones.

The king had seen the power of Daniel's God. He was so moved that he wrote these words to all who lived in his kingdom:

"Peace to you! Let everyone in my kingdom tremble and fear before Daniel's God. He is the living God. He alone lives forever. His kingdom will never be destroyed, and He will rule until the end. He saves and rescues. He works signs and wonders in heaven and on earth. He saved Daniel from the power of the lions."

So, despite the evil plans of the leaders of Babylon, Daniel blossomed all the more during the reign of Darius.

This story may have you thinking of another man, centuries later, who defeated all-but-certain death. He, too, was placed in a den-like tomb with a rock against the opening. He, too, received a punishment He did not deserve. And when He did the impossible, it brought many to faith in God.

If you're thinking of Jesus, you are correct! Daniel is one of the most important figures in the Bible, not only because he's brave and courageous, but because he helps us look forward to someone greater—Jesus. We see hints of Jesus in Daniel when he...

... is sent to another country (Jesus was sent to Egypt shortly after birth).
... remains faithful to God in the face of evil.
... prays consistently to God.
... speaks confidently to leaders, even though harm awaits him.

Can you think of other ways that Daniel reminds us of Jesus?

Kaleidoscope Corner
Seeing Jesus in the Old Testament

From the first to the last page, all of the Bible celebrates Jesus. He was with His Father at creation in Genesis 1. Likewise, the final page of the Bible says over and over that Jesus is "coming soon."

All the pages between Genesis 1 and Revelation 22 point us to the beauty of Jesus. These stories, such as the one we just read, show us a familiar pattern of sin and salvation that finds its best and ultimate answer in Jesus' death and resurrection. Consider some other stories and how they point us to Jesus. Ask yourself these questions:

- Is sin a part of this story or passage?
- Do you see God's kindness, goodness, and mercy?
- How does this story make our hearts long for Jesus? Where do we see our need for His perfect life, death, and resurrection?

Our favorite passages:

- Genesis 4:1-16
- 2 Samuel 7:1-17
- Psalms 23
- Jonah 1-3

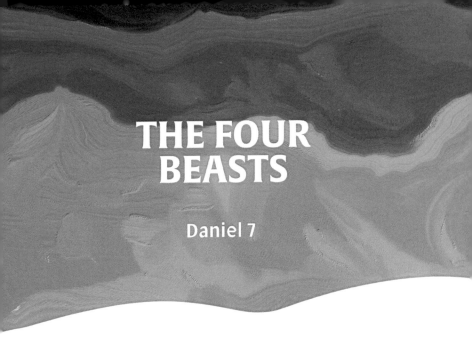

THE FOUR BEASTS

Daniel 7

Dear Reader,

I'm delighted you've made it to this point! Daniel is a very challenging book, no matter how old you are. Well done! Before we start this last section of Daniel, I want you to know two things:

1. Daniel 7-12 is a fast finish to the book! Daniel tries to cover hundreds of years of history in just a few chapters. If it feels like there is a lot to take in and you don't quite understand everything, that's okay! As long as you walk away knowing the three promises at the end of Chapter 12, you are well on your way to understanding the whole point of the book of Daniel.
2. The events of Daniel 7-12 may seem scary. But, you should know that 99% of the things you're about to read have already happened. You don't have to worry that they will happen again. In fact, for those who trust in Jesus, our best days are still ahead of us!

With that, let's jump in!

Over the years, Daniel had some dreams of his own. One of those dreams came during the first year of Belshazzar's reign in Babylon. After he awoke, Daniel wrote down what he saw.

"I saw the wind coming from the north, south, east, and west, stirring up the sea," Daniel began. "Then, splashing out of the sea came four great beasts.

"The first was like a lion with wings like an eagle. But then I looked, and its wings fell to the side as it stood on two feet like a man and took on the mind of a human.

"The second beast was like a bear. One side of the bear was larger and more powerful than the other. In its mouth were three ribs. A voice told the bear, 'Get up, destroy, and eat as much as you want.'

"Then there was a leopard with four wings on its back. Curiously, it also had four heads. This beast was very powerful!

"After that, I saw a fourth beast. He was terrifying and powerful (even stronger than the first three!). It had iron teeth, which he used to devour what he pleased. Whatever was left behind, it stamped down with its feet. This last beast was quite different than the first three and had ten horns.

"And if you looked closely, there was an eleventh horn, a little one, which came up and destroyed three of the first ten horns. And if you looked at the little horn even closer, you'd see the horn had eyes like the eyes of a man and a mouth which boasted of its power."

What a terrifyingly horrid dream! But then a ray of hope burst into Daniel's imagination.

"I looked up from the beasts, and I saw thrones as you'd see in a palace. And then I saw Him—the Ancient of Days—the One who's in charge of time itself, God Almighty. He took His seat on the throne. His clothing was white as snow, and His hair was like pure wool, glowing in perfection!

"And then, a stream of fire erupted, and His throne sprouted wheels like a fiery chariot-mobile! Thousands upon thousands of angels served Him, and hundreds of thousands stood before Him.

"Then, the books of all the good and evil of all those on earth were opened.

"Now, over in the corner, the little horn of the fourth beast was boasting of its greatness. The next instant, though, he was killed, and his body was burned in the fire. As for the other three beasts, their power was taken away, but they were allowed to live for a season of time.

"Then, coming down from the clouds, I saw someone who was both human and God. He went to the Ancient of Days, and it seemed like they knew each other."

Daniel continued, "The Ancient of Days made Him a ruler and gave Him power and glory so that all the people would serve Him; and that His rule would last forever and His kingdom would not be destroyed."

Can you imagine what Daniel must have felt at this moment? He held in his mind a vision as hopeful as it was scary. But, little did he know, this vision was a window into the future of the world.

Daniel approached someone to help him understand this dream. What the helper shared sparked faith and trust deep in Daniel's soul.

"The four beasts you saw are four evil kings who will come to rule the earth," the dream helper began. "But, those who love God will live in His kingdom forever and ever."

This news was excellent, but Daniel was still most curious about the fourth beast—the one with all the horns.

"Oh, that beast!" the dream helper remarked. "The fourth beast is a monstrous kingdom that is not like the other kingdoms. It will devour the whole earth and trample it down as it breaks it to pieces.

"The ten horns are ten kings who will lead this kingdom. One of the horns, the little one, will rise and kill three of his fellow kings. The little one will speak evil against the Most High God and will be a pain in the neck to those who follow God. But he will be judged by God and will lose his strength.

"Then, the saints of the Most High God will receive the power and greatness of all the kingdoms of the earth. Those who love Him will enjoy Him forever and ever, and all His people will serve and obey Him."

Daniel heard all of this and knew that, ultimately, it was good news for God's people. But he also understood that a tremendous amount of terrifying evil would come to the earth.

This shocking news made the color drain from his face as he kept the matter to himself and told nobody what he knew.

THE GOAT & THE RAM

Daniel 8

Two years later, Daniel had another mysterious vision. Let's listen to him tell us about it...

"I saw a ram on the side of a river. It had two horns, but one horn was longer than the other. The ram charged northward, southward, and westward. No man or beast could stop him. He did whatever he pleased.

"Then, from the west, a male goat bolted across the face of the whole earth. It was floating, as its feet didn't even touch the ground. He had one very curious-looking horn between his eyes.

"The floating goat ran toward the ram with all his power. Both the ram's horns fell to the ground, and he had no power against the mighty goat.

"After this, the goat grew very strong. His one horn fell to the ground, and four more horns grew in its place. These four horns pointed toward the four winds of heaven.

"Out of one of the horns grew another little horn. This little horn fought against the south, the east, and even toward the Promised Land. It even became violent against those who loved the Lord and killed many people.

"The little horn seemed to grow even as great as God as it took over the Sanctuary and places of worship.

"But then I heard a holy voice speaking, 'How long will this evil last?' And another voice replied, 'For 2,300 evenings and mornings (which is 6 years). Then the Sanctuary will return to its glory."

Daniel wanted to understand this vision, so an angel named Gabriel came to explain all he'd seen. But Daniel became frightened when he saw the angel and fell on his face.

But the angel spoke gently, saying, "Daniel, this vision is about what is to come. The ram you saw, the one with the two horns, these horns are the kings of Media and Persia who have come to capture Babylon. The goat is the king of Greece. The one horn the goat had at the beginning was the first king. Then the four horns are four kingdoms who will come out of Greece after defeating Media and Persia. But these four kingdoms will not be as strong as the first kingdom.

"The little horn, which came off one of the four horns, is a king who will arise at the end of the kingdom. He will cause destruction and great evil. He will kill those who believe in God. He will even rise up against God.

"But in the end, he will be broken—but not by a human hand. God will remove his power."

Daniel was overcome with the news of what was to come. It was more than he could handle to know about the suffering that was to come over the next six years. The pressure made him sick, and he lay in bed for days.

DANIEL'S PRAYER

Daniel 9

Daniel read Jeremiah's writings in the first year that Darius the Mede ruled as king. The Bible we know today was still forming, but the book of Jeremiah was well known.

As he read, Daniel, now an 80-year-old man, was reminded that the punishment of exile for God's people was to last 70 years (Jer. 25:11). Daniel looked around him, though, and realized that as 70 years drew to a close, not much had changed.

God's people were still just as sinful as their neighbors.

So, Daniel prayed to the Lord. He begged for mercy while he fasted from eating, wore sackcloth, and covered his body in ashes—all signs of repentance, a turning from sin.

"O Lord," Daniel prayed, "the great and awesome God, who keeps His promises and loves those who keep His commandments with an everlasting love, we have sinned and done wrong and acted wickedly. We have rebelled and ignored Your commandments and rules."

Let's pause and notice some things about Daniel's prayer. First of all, Daniel loves God. Like, really, really loves God! Everything around Daniel is evil and falling apart, and yet he says that God is "great and awesome."

Second, Daniel uses the word "we" instead of "I." Daniel is not only confessing his sin but also the sin of the people of Israel. He is a humble leader of God's people.

Third, Daniel doesn't sugarcoat the truth. Daniel doesn't say they have "forgotten" or "lost sight of" God's commandments. Instead, he uses stronger words like "rebelled" and "ignored." Daniel understands that God already knows the truth. There's no use in hiding and only freedom to be found in honesty.

His prayer continued, "We've not listened to Your servants and prophets, who spoke in Your name to our kings, princes, fathers, and all the people.

"You, O Lord, are righteous. But, to us belongs open shame: the men of Judah, those who lived in the city of Jerusalem and all of Israel have been taken from our homes to far-away lands because of our sin. To us belongs open shame: to our kings, princes, and our fathers, because we have sinned against You.

"The Lord is merciful and forgiving, for we have rebelled against Him and have not obeyed the voice of the Lord our God. We have not walked in His laws, which He showed us through His servants and prophets.

"All Israel has broken Your law and turned away. We have refused to obey You. The punishment Moses spoke of long ago has come to us because of our sin.

"God has kept His word. He's never punished anyone like He's punished His people. But, we still have not changed. We have not turned from our sin. We have not sought God. We have not learned," Daniel prayed.

Daniel reminded himself and others, "He is the God who brought our people out of Egypt and back home to Jerusalem with His mighty hand. Now, with the same hand, He swept us far from home because of our sin.

"O our Lord, according to Your righteousness (not ours!), remove Your anger from Jerusalem, Your holy hill. Bring the exile to an end. Make Your face shine on Your Sanctuary once again!

"O Lord, listen; O Lord, forgive. O Lord, pay attention and act."

While Daniel was praying, the angel Gabriel came to him again with the message, "O Daniel, I have come to help you understand, for you are greatly loved. Know this: God has a perfect amount of time in place from now until Jerusalem is rebuilt and restored as your home. Then the anointed prince (who we know as Jesus) will come. But He will be killed, and after that, destruction will come for Jerusalem."

GREATLY LOVED

Daniel 10

Sometime later, Daniel had yet another vision. The vision was so overwhelmingly sad that Daniel could hardly eat or drink for three weeks. But the vision was only one reason for Daniel's grief.

Little by little, the Israelites were returning to the Promised Land by this point in the story. Yet, Daniel remained in Babylon. Because of his position and age, it was unlikely he'd ever return home.

When you add that stress to the weight of Israel's sin and Daniel's knowledge of what was to come for God's people, his sadness makes sense. Can you imagine being Daniel?! What a challenging life!

But, as we will see very soon, those who walk through great tragedy often experience great closeness with God as He longs to be with the brokenhearted.

After the vision, sorrowful Daniel was standing on the bank of a river. Suddenly, out of the corner of his eye, he saw a man clothed in linen, with a belt of beautiful gold around his waist. His body looked like polished stone, and his face flashed with lightning. His eyes were flames of fire. His legs were like bronze, and his voice echoed powerfully around the river bed.

Just the sight of this man brought Daniel to his knees. All Daniel's strength left his body as the color drained from his face. Daniel fell into a deep sleep.

Then the man with the gold belt and lightning face reached down and touched Daniel as he spoke the words Daniel's heart needed, "O Daniel, you are greatly loved. Stand. Listen to my words."

The words were enough to bring Daniel to his feet while his arms and legs trembled uncontrollably, not knowing what this man would say next.

"Fear not, Daniel," the man began. "From the first day that you understood the good news of God and followed Him with your whole heart, God has heard your words.

"I would have come sooner, but an evil angel blocked me. You should know that there's a real, spiritual battle alongside the battles you see between people! And now I have come to tell you what will happen to Israel."

Daniel was dumbfounded. He could only stare at the ground, unable to speak.

But then, the man touched Daniel's lips. Once again, Daniel was able to speak, saying, "The visions I've seen are so painful. I have lost all my strength. How can I speak with you when I can hardly breathe?"

Then, once more, the bronze-legged, stone-bodied man touched Daniel and gave him strength as he spoke these words, "O Daniel, you are greatly loved. Do not fear. Peace be with you. Be strong and of good courage."

Finally, Daniel felt his strength return as the man continued, "Do you know why I've come to you, Daniel? I'm here so you will know you're not alone, even though scary things surround you. Our God will defend His people. Even now, when I leave you, I will return to fight against the evil Persians. After the Persians, I will protect God's people against the next nation, which is Greece.

"But know this, Daniel. God has written the book of truth. In this book is His plan for the world. No matter how terrifying, nothing that happens is outside of His control. God has sent His angels, Michael and myself, to strengthen you and all of God's people."

Who was this man dressed in linen, and why does he enter the story at this point? He offered Daniel comfort with his words and presence when he needed it most.

As we read further in the Bible, we learn that this man is Jesus (see a very similar description in Revelation 1:13-16). He makes a special appearance in the book of Daniel!

It's calming and reassuring to know that someone in charge knows the way forward in scary times. Think about it—when there's a frightening thunderstorm outside, it's reassuring to hear an adult say, "This storm is bad, but it won't last much longer."

The book of Daniel was given to God's people to strengthen them in troublesome times. Jesus' presence with Daniel gave him the calm assurance that God controls all things.

Kaleidoscope Corner
Lip Touching

In the last chapter, Daniel became so overwhelmed with sadness that he couldn't speak. Then, an angel touched his lips, and he could speak once more.

This is not the first time a prophet, or messenger of God, experienced something like this.

In the sixth chapter of Isaiah, the prophet Isaiah finally speaks. He says that he is a "man of unclean lips, and he lives with people who have unclean lips." Isaiah knew his sin and felt the weight of his words!

Just then, an angelic being, known as a seraphim, touched Isaiah's lips with a burning coal while saying, "Your guilt is taken away, and your sin is atoned for." Only then was Isaiah able to speak to God.

Likewise, the prophet Jeremiah told God he could not be a prophet in the first chapter of his book. Hearing that, God touched Jeremiah's lips and gave him the ability to speak as a prophet, even though he was just a small boy.

This small but important moment shows us at least two things about Daniel:

1. Daniel was a great leader because he was aware of his sin and the sin of Israel.
2. Daniel was a prophet, not because it was his idea, but because God gave him the job. As if it were not already clear by this point in the book, the lip touching was one more sign that Daniel was God's chosen leader.

SHINE LIKE STARS

Daniel 11-12

The man clothed in linen from the last chapter strengthened Daniel with a final message of what the future held, "Fighting and violence will fill our land for hundreds of years. It won't be pretty, but I want you and the people of God to know so that they will trust in God's promises even in the worst of times.

"Soon, three other kings will come to power in Persia, replacing you. After them, a fourth one will appear. He will have more money and wealth than any of those before him. When he senses that his power and riches have reached their peak, he'll go to war against the entire kingdom of Greece.

"But then a mighty king will arise in Greece (this is the male goat from Daniel 8). He will take over everything. Every land. Every river. Everything. He will do as he pleases."

The man continued, "But, at the very height of his power, when everything seems like it's under control, the once mighty kingdom will split into four parts, like the four points of a compass (like the four horns of the goat).

"But none of his children will have any power over these four parts. Instead, other power-hungry people will take whatever they can manage to get their hands on.

"At first, the king of the south will grow strong, and one of his princes will become even stronger than him. Then, together they will try to make peace with the king of the north. But that peace won't last long.

"Then, year after year, the kings of the north and the kings of the south will fight one another in battle after battle after battle. The world, during this time, will be controlled by a bunch of power-hungry, war-mongering, bloodthirsty rulers.

"And then, a hateful ruler will come to power (this is likely the little horn from Chapter 8). He will not receive power from anyone. Instead, he will take it by force and bribes.

"This will be a difficult time for God's people. The new ruler will make people worship new gods. The Israelites' faith will face test after test during this time. Home won't look much like home as the king will even make the Sanctuary a place to make fun of God. The king will become friends with others who've turned their backs on God.

"Through all of this, even though God's people will die and lose their homes and possessions, God will sustain them. They will grow in love as they see that the Lord is good.

"In the end, the king of the south will attack, but his forces will be no match. So the king of the north will rush south like a tornado, with chariots and horsemen, and even with ships at sea.

"The hateful ruler will even reach far south to Egypt, where he will steal gold, silver, and treasures.

"But then reports will come from the north and east that will throw the ruler into a panic. As soon as he rushes to stomp down the threat, he'll meet his end. Nobody will be around to help.

"At this time, Michael, who's been the champion of your people, will come to the rescue. The world will be in chaos when Michael arrives. But God will save His people, every last one whose name is in the book."

Let's pause for a moment. History tells us that real people and nations actually end up doing exactly what the book of Daniel predicts.

But here's the good news for the children of God in Daniel's day—though there are dark times ahead, the future is far more beautiful than we can imagine.

The man explained explained further, "In the last days, everyone who has died will wake up. Those who are children of God will rise to eternal life. They will shine like stars forever.

"However, those who are not children of God will rise to eternal destruction and shame."

After he finished, Daniel sealed these words in a book to wait until the end of time (See Revelation 20 for when these books reappear!).

As Daniel took in the scene, two men appeared. One of them stood on one side of the river and the other on the opposite side. Then the man dressed in linen floated above the water between the two.

One of the first two men asked the third, "How long will this story go on?"

Then the man in linen raised both his hands toward heaven, saying, "Some time will pass, but God will bring evil to an end."

Daniel was confused, asking, "I don't understand. Can you tell me the secrets of the end?"

But he would get no answer, only these promises, recorded as the last words of the book of Daniel:

Faithful and wicked people will live side by side until the end of time.

Those who trust God do not need to worry. They can rest in comfort and safety, even when the world is scary. Just like Jesus showed up in the book of Daniel to give him courage, Jesus also guards your heart and mind and gives you His peace. Our God will defend His people!

Finally, our God is in charge of time. He is the Ancient of Days. He alone knows when Jesus will return to make all things new, and it will be at just the right time.